BRITAIN

KING'S NORTON
PAST & PRESENT

WENDY PEARSON

SUTTON PUBLISHING

Sutton Publishing Limited
Phoenix Mill · Thrupp · Stroud
Gloucestershire · GL5 2BU

First published 2004

Title page photograph: The Saracen's Head, 1906.

British Library Cataloguing in Publication Data
A catalogue record for this book is available from the British Library.

ISBN 0-7509-3858-7

Typeset in 10.5/13.5 Photina.
Typesetting and origination by
Sutton Publishing Limited.
Printed and bound in England by
J.H. Haynes & Co. Ltd, Sparkford.

Drawing of the east side of the parish church of St Nicolas from where the library now stands, *c.* 1880. Unusually for work of this quality the sketch is unsigned.

CONTENTS

The Mop, 1982. On this occasion the fair was held in front of King's Norton cinema.

KING'S NORTON HISTORY SOCIETY

The Society has 40–50 members and meets regularly on the last Monday in the month, from September to May, in the Saracen's Head, for talks on a variety of subjects. The Society originated from an Extra-mural Study Group organised in the 1960s by Miss P.A. Nicklin. Stephen Price, with his significant research, ensured the continuing study of the history of King's Norton, in the 1970s. The research, using the tithe map, the investigation into the purchase of the Manor from King George, and other studies, needed to be formally recorded. In 1980 Helen Goodger, Myra Watson and Stephen Price held a public meeting in King's Norton library, and the King's Norton History Society was formed.

In 1982 the Society persuaded Birmingham Civic Society to put up a plaque on the Old Grammar School to commemorate the seventeenth-century schoolmaster Thomas Hall. Funds were raised, by holding a stall at King's Norton Carnival from 1983 to 1985 and other grants, to purchase a new signboard for the Saracen's Head. Lord King's Norton unveiled this in 1986. A two-day exhibition was held in Bell's Farm in 1989 in connection with the Maypole May Festival.

The committee has organised local walks and visits to places of interest. James Melling's conducted tours of the Saracen's Head, the Old Grammar School, and church visits were very well supported. Audrey Langston is largely responsible for organising annual coach tours for the Society. There have been two walks round the medieval boundary of King's Norton. The first was inspired by Frances Hopkins in 1989 and the second by Greta Lacey in 2002.

The Society is a member of the Birmingham & District Local History Association. It participates in open days organised by Birmingham City Council as well as in events run by St Nicolas Church. Exhibitions and tours of the Saracen's Head attract many visitors. There is a trail round the village green that describes the changes and developments both ancient and within living memory.

The Society has published ten pamphlets of the interests and research of its members. These are *King's Norton's Wastes and Commons* by F. Hopkins; *Notes on the History of King's Norton* by H. Goodger; *Cotteridge and its Churches before 1911* by F. Hopkins; *The Boundary of King's Norton* by F. Hopkins; *Boyhood Memories of King's Norton* by F. Clulee; *Learning Began Here* by K. Knowles; *On Looking Back* by Jessie Oliver; *Josiah Mason: Innovative Birmingham Industrialist and Philanthropic Giant* by D. Hazzard; *The Rev. Thomas Hall of King's Norton: A Birmingham Pastor in Civil War and Revolution* by F. Hopkins and D. Hazzard; *Birmingham, Chartism, and the Chartist Village of Dodford* by D. Hazzard.

James Melling has done substantial research on King's Norton, especially on the architecture of the older buildings. He has published several books, which include *The Changing Times in King's Norton, St Nicolas – King's Norton, The Saracen's Head, The Junction House* and *The Old Grammar School*. Other publications include *King's Norton* by Helen Goodger and *King's Norton* by Pauline Caswell.

INTRODUCTION

Archaeological surveys beside Longdales Road in 2002 confirmed the presence of a Romano-British farmstead in King's Norton. The site, chosen for a new cemetery, is particularly important, as it is one of very few settlements from the Roman period known in the Birmingham area. Evidence connects the site to Icknield Street, a Roman road, which runs from Alcester through King's Norton to the Metchley Fort, and then on to Wall.

There was probably a minor settlement in King's Norton during Saxon times. The entry for Worcestershire in Domesday Book of 1086 starts with the king's own lands, firstly, Bromsgrove with eighteen berewicks or outlying hamlets. King's Norton was the hamlet north of Bromsgrove that belonged to the king. The Subsidy Rolls of 1327 records fifty-three people with sufficient property to be taxed in defence of the kingdom against the Scots.

In the Middle Ages Manor Courts dealing with minor law cases for Bromsgrove and King's Norton were held every three weeks at 'the Lickey'. The ancient manor of King's Norton included the modern districts of Balsall Heath, Moseley, King's Heath, West Heath, Wythall, Rednal, and parts of Rubery. In 1564 Queen Elizabeth sold the Manor of Bromsgrove but King's Norton remained Crown property until George III sold it, in 1804, to John Taylor of Moseley Hall.

During the monarch's ownership, King's Norton was often granted to the queen consort. In 1643, during the Civil War, Henrietta Maria, wife of Charles I, spent a night at King's Norton when leading troops to reinforce the king's army at Oxford. It is reasonable to expect her to stay in the most important house. Popular legend suggests she slept in what is now called the Queen's Room in the Saracen's Head.

Thomas Hall took the position of schoolmaster at the Free Grammar School in King's Norton in 1629. As he supported government by Parliament the presence of the queen and Royalist troops must have been a difficult time for him and his followers. Following the execution of the king in 1649 and during the rule of Cromwell, Thomas Hall wrote the first book known to have been published in Birmingham. The Act of Uniformity ended his ministry. He died in 1665 having made known his wish to be buried in the churchyard. The whereabouts of his grave is unknown.

In 1616 King's Norton was granted a charter to hold a fair or 'Mop', a tradition that still continues. The township obviously prospered as evidenced by the successive enlargements of the parish church which was dedicated to St Nicolas. There were some very fine timbered buildings around the Green. The buildings now known as the Saracen's Head, the Old Grammar School, and the Spar supermarket were built in the fifteenth century.

King's Norton had been a rural area with the classic English setting of a village around a green. Much of the land surrounding the village was agricultural, and this was recorded in the 1840 tithe map. The River Rea supported Wychall Mill, Hurst Mill and Lifford Mill on its route through the present-day King's Norton. The station at King's Norton is thought to be one of the earliest in Birmingham. The Birmingham to Worcester canal runs through the Wasthill Tunnel, which at 2,726 yards is the fourth longest in the country.

Agricultural change and the Enclosures Act resulted in migration from the country to the city. The density of people through infilling and the building of back-to-back housing resulted in concerns for health and sanitation. The Artisans' Dwelling Act and slum clearance created the need to extend the city boundaries to build more homes.

In the nineteenth century Balsall Heath broke away from King's Norton and became part of Birmingham; in 1898 the Urban District of Northfield and King's Norton was created, and in 1911 the north of King's Norton became part of Birmingham. Urbanisation was rapid with the building of new estates to cater for the needs of families moved out of the city with the clearance of slums. Rosalind Dickers very well expresses this change in a poem:

'Time Remembered'

Oh, how I would like to see King's Norton like it used to be.
Our proud old Church, it still stands there
Against the trees, so stark and bare.
Do you remember, or have you read,
The cottages around the Old Bull's Head,
The workhouses with bricks of red and grey,
Where tramps used their weary heads to lay.
Five pubs there were, perhaps too many,
A pint of ale for just one penny.
The cattle market, where once a week
Farmers came to sell their sheep.
Hough's Brickyard, down Ardath road,
Great shire horses pulled their heavy load.
And came October, in the Fall
The hiring Mop gave us a call.
The roasted ox with meat so sweet,
Kiddies dancing in the street,
The greasy pole, and prancing horses,
The sound of Showmen's raucous voices.
Do you remember – I do – still
The old flour mill down the hill,
The wheel a-turning in waters green,
A prettier sight you've never seen.
A Mint there was, or so I'm told,
Where we stamped our pennies bold.
Up Masshouse Lane a donkey track
Past pigsties and fine haystacks.
The two mile tunnel, dark and long,
The Bargemen's feet propelled the boats along.
Alas, alas, those days have gone,
Great tower blocks now we gaze upon.

Some of the tower blocks have since been demolished. Thanks to the efforts of conservationists in the 'Battle of the Swing Bridge' the canals are navigable, and the towpath had been made available for walkers and cyclists. The love of steam engines is kept alive with the 'Thomas the Tank Engine' books written by Rev. W. Awdry when he was a curate in King's Norton. The village community is vibrant and thriving with its many groups based at the Saracen's Head, where the Parish Office is also located. Despite all the changes King's Norton still retains its unique and traditional English characteristics of a village with a green.

1

The Centre of the Village

The Saracen's Head, St Nicolas Church, and the old cottages on 'Twatling',
photographed by Sir Benjamin Stover in 1868. The centre of King's Norton is the area
surrounding the Village Green as identified in the 1969 Conservation Order. In 1854
J. Noake, in *The Rambler in Worcestershire*, wrote, 'Passing through the churchyard by
this house [The Saracen's Head] you come at once into the centre of the village – a
kind of triangle or square of time-worn buildings, with a patch of green turf in the
centre, where pigs, and geese, and donkeys, and boys with their hoops, and little girls
with babies nearly as heavy as themselves, have rejoiced in rustic felicity from time
immemorial. The ancient appearance of the village is remarkable.'

West view of St Nicolas Church, photographed by J.M.L. Aston, 1870. The church is a very distinctive building and along with the Saracen's Head, the Old Grammar School and the other properties belonging to the Parish Church Council, have been subjects for many artists, and photographers.

Postcard of St Nicolas, with a 1905 postmark. The church building has a long history, dating back to Norman times. There is no evidence linking the church to the Crusades. The present tower and crocketed spire were built during the fifteenth century at a time when large houses were being built around the Green. As can be expected there have been additions and modifications that reflect the growing wealth of the village. Behind the idyllic setting, though, there was a division between the rich and the poor. The decline in available labourers, as a consequence of the Black Death in 1348, may have led to a change from working the farms to grazing sheep. Unemployment and poverty caused more vagrants to wander the countryside, and the Parish enforced laws to return them to their place of birth. The king owned the Forest of Feckenham, which surrounded much of the adjacent land. Hunting for deer and wild boar was illegal, and poachers were severely punished.

The north side of King's Norton Green, 2002.

The north side of the Green in a drawing from the *Yellow Pages* by James Priddey. In 1840 there was cause for concern about the stability of the spire. A local blacksmith was called in to make a nut to clamp the rod supporting the spire to wooden beams placed across the tower. As the screwing process took place a villager ran up to the belfry to say that the top of the spire was being turned. A delightful fairytale was told that when carrying out urgent repairs to the tower jewellery was found in the nests of the jackdaws, and this was sold to recoup the costs.

St Nicolas Church lych gate at the dedication ceremony, 1922. A bronze plaque inscribed with the names of all those who gave their lives during the First World War was placed inside the lych gate. A second plaque has since been added to commemorate those from King's Norton who perished during the Second World War.

The old vicarage, built in 1860. The Revd Joseph Amphlett was Assistant Curate of Bromsgrove in charge of the much larger parish of King's Norton, Wythall and Balsall Heath from 1827 to 1847. He then became the first vicar of King's Norton. The vicar lived in a house at the top of Parson's Hill until this large Victorian Gothic vicarage was built in 1860.

Building the new vicarage, 1969. This vicarage was built in 1969 as a home for the Revd A.J. Balmforth and his family. He was vicar from 1965 to 1979.

Inside the church is this marble plaque to John Middlemore. Near the lych gate is a late eighteenth-century memorial to the Middlemore family. This memorial is a reminder of a family that was rich and powerful from the sixteenth to the nineteenth centuries. In the record of proceedings at the King's Norton Manorial Court in 1596 there is an entry stating that George Middlemore of Hazelwell was fined 20 shillings because he 'harboured, supported, and comforted sturdy beggars in his house against the Laws of the Kingdom'. The memorial is now a Grade II listed building.

Grevis family memorials outside the south wall of St Nicolas Church, photographed in 1982. Sir Richard Grevis was High Sheriff of Worcester and Deputy Lieutenant to His Majesty in Wales. He was a well-known Justice of the Peace for many years. He died in 1632 and his wife, Lady Anne, died in 1653. In St Nicolas Church there is an alabaster relief tomb to Sir Richard and Lady Ann his wife.

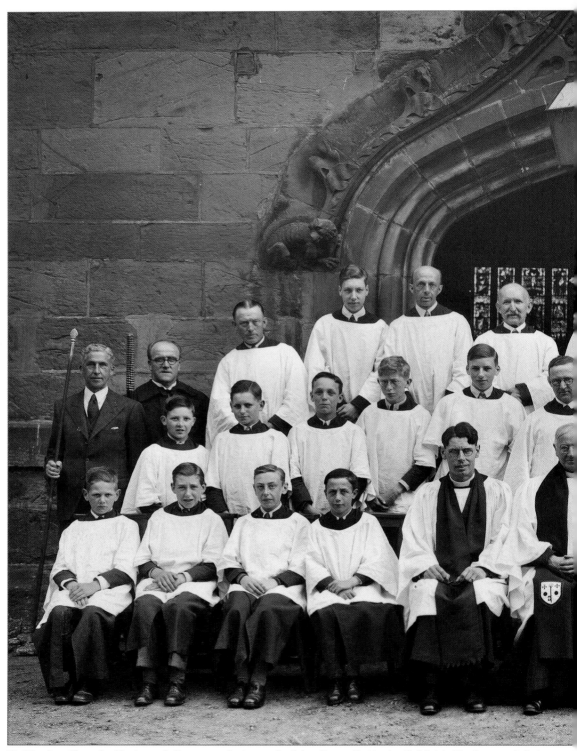

St Nicolas Church Choir and Servers, photographed by Percy Bott, April 1944. Back row, left to right: W.J. Holton, Edward Blake, Mr Berman, Roy Yates, Mr Peplow, -?-, Mr Hems, Mr Young, C.A.P. Rogers, Mr Millard, John Whitton. Middle row: -?-, Philip Haycock, Anthony Phillips, Norman

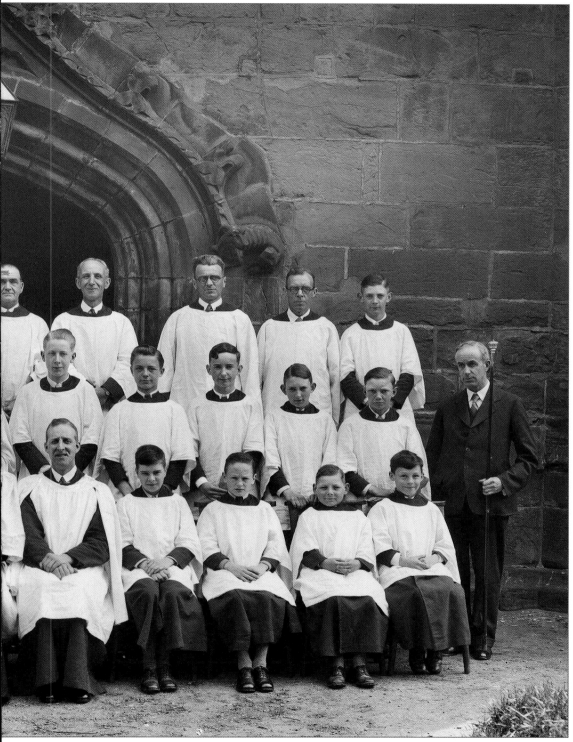

Millard, Eric Meek, George Yates, Rex Clarke, Peter Eborn, Christopher Pendleton, Philip Matkin, -?-, Ernest Greenhill. Front row: John Oliver, Brian Hall, Trevor Dawson, -?-, the Revd Wilbert Awdry, Canon Thomas Shelton Dunn, W. Reginald Masters, Geoffrey Nottley, -?-, -?-, Maurice Eaton.

St Nicolas Sunday School outing, 1920s.

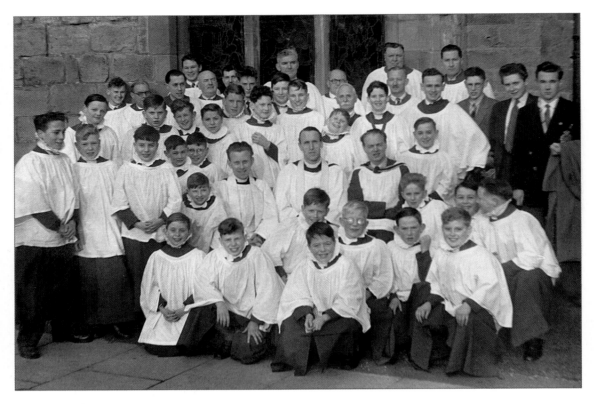

St Nicolas Church Choir, 1956–7.

The Revd Charles William Barnard, the vicar, and his family, 1908.

Congratulatory dinner held at the Saracen's Head
to mark the eightieth birthday of Mr Josiah Hands,
19 January 1909.

Congratulatory Dinner

.. TO ..

MR. JOSIAH HANDS

ON ATTAINING HIS

EIGHTIETH BIRTHDAY.

JANUARY 19TH, 1909.

Chairman, CANON BARNARD (Vicar of Kings Norton).

MENU.

COD.   OYSTER SAUCE

———

BARON OF BEEF.

———

BOILED LEGS OF MUTTON.

———

ROAST TURKEY.

———

PLUM PUDDINGS.

———

MINCE PIES.

———

CHEESE.   CELERY.

TOASTS.

"THE KING,"   ...   ...   THE VICAR.

NATIONAL ANTHEM.

Solo, MR E. A JAMES.

"OUR GUEST," ...   ... A. STANFORD

SONG :

" A Fine Old English Gentleman,"

MR. E. A. JAMES

"THE CHAIRMAN,"

J. S. PRITCHETT, C.C.

———

GLEES & SONGS,

THE ST. NICHOLAS QUARTETTE.

Messrs. T. G Smith, J. W. Vincent,

E. A. James, L. Dunn.

Humorist   ...   ...   MR. WORRALL.

The Menu and Toasts for the dinner. Mr Hands was Registrar of Births and Deaths for the
parish for twenty-five years. He succeeded his father-in-law in this position, from which he
retired in 1908. Before that he was Postmaster of King's Norton. He was born in the village
and took an active interest in most local institutions and affairs.

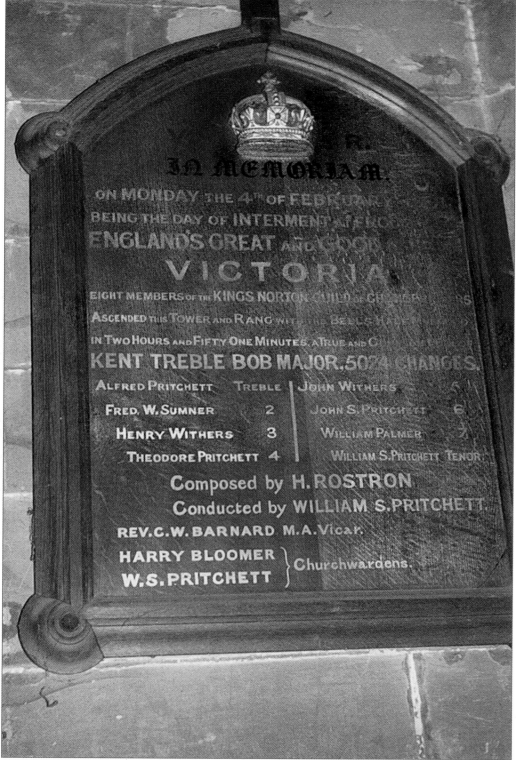

Memorial peal for Queen Victoria, as described on this plaque inside the bell tower, 1982.

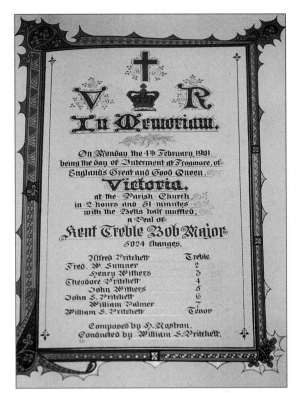

Above left: The bellringers' room in the tower, 1982. In 1903 visiting bellringers set a world record of change ringing. Eight men from other churches locked themselves in the tower and rang peals for eight and a half hours non-stop. During this time 14,112 changes were completed.

Above right: In Memoriam Victoria. Ringing master, Ray Aldington, made available the record book of certificates of special peals rung in commemoration of significant events, including the death of Queen Victoria, and the restoration of peace in South Africa.

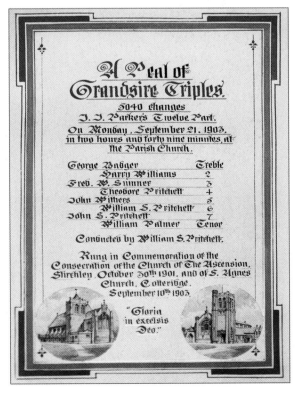

The peal of grandsire triples rung in commemoration of the consecration of the Church of the Ascension and St Agnes Church includes images of the sister churches, both of which have since been demolished.

The Old Grammar School from the church tower. Thomas Hall, 1610–65, is the best-remembered master of the Old Grammar School to which he attracted pupils from all over England and Ireland. His opinion on the purpose of cosmetics is a good example of his view: 'to inamour and ensnare others, and to kindle a fire and flame of lust in the hearts of those who cast their eyes on them'. He suffered greatly during the Civil War for his puritan beliefs (King's Norton was Royalist). He was cursed, plundered and imprisoned. He wrote many books and treatises, 270 of which were left to King's Norton. Ejected in 1662 by the Act of Uniformity, his career was finished. He was buried in the churchyard, by his own wish 'amongst the common people', in 1665. No known grave exists. In 1861 the upper floor was opened as a girls' school. Ellen Summers, who was related to the Shephard family, was a well-loved mistress of the Old Grammar School from 1865 to 1880.

The Old Grammar School, 2002. The change of access to the upper floor had been made by 1930.

Opposite left: The Old Grammar School, 1899. The school dates back to the middle of the fifteenth century. The upper storey appears to be considerably older than the lower storey suggesting it was initially raised on stilts, and the ground floor was filled in later to provide further accommodation. It is probable that it was originally a Chantry School. In the Middle Ages, linked with the doctrine of Purgatory, it was believed that the prayers of the living could benefit the souls of the dead. The prosperous country gentry endowed land whose rents were paid for a priest to say daily masses for the founders' souls. In many cases, the priests were directed to educate poor boys and could also take paying pupils. The building is currently on the English Heritage 'at risk' registers.

Restoration Winners

In May 2004 the Parish Church Council made public the news that the Old Grammar School and the Saracen's Head were to feature in the BBC2 *Restoration* project. In each of the seven programmes three buildings on the English Heritage 'Buildings at Risk' register would be presented.

Viewers then had the opportunity of voting, by making a telephone call, for the building they wanted to be rescued. Each phone call contributed 34 pence to the fund. The winner from each programme, along with the overall runner-up, went into a final round on 8 August 2004 staged at Hampton Court Palace. The £2.5 million grant from the Heritage Lottery Fund was considerably increased by the 750,000 calls that were made. The King's Norton buildings received 113,326 votes and won just over £3 million to begin the restoration of the Old Grammar School and the Saracen's Head. The delighted Canon Rob Morris gives his thanks to everyone who supported the campaign.

The Saracen's Head, 1906.

The Saracen's Head, *c.* 1930. The building called the Saracen's Head is actually a combination of structures. The long north wing on the right of the frontage is thought to have originated as a high status wool stapler's residence. It was built in the winter of 1491–2. As dried oak is extremely hard the oak used for the building would have been freshly cut. It was therefore possible, using dendrochronology, to give a very specific date when it was built. Part of the east wing was probably a separate building constructed about ten years later.

During the Victorian period the buildings were joined and the south wing added. The courtyard looks like the setting for a Shakespearean play. Good stabling was advertised at the inn. In 1840 there was a licence for a public house. In 1890 the building was bought by Atkinson's Brewery. It was sold to Mitchells & Butlers in 1918 and they, in turn, gave it to the Parish Council in 1930.

The front ground floor was a grocery and hardware shop. By 1906 it had become Ye Olde Village Tea Room, although photographs show that this had been closed by 1931. The last licensee of the Saracen's Head as a public house was George Coombes. Later in the twentieth century the vergers of the church lived in the north wing. The last three resident vergers were Mr Blake, Mr Davy and Mr Nerding.

Much needed restoration work began in 1972 and continued during the 1980s. More work is now needed to overcome the restricted access and facilities.

Restoration Proposals
It is intended that the Old Grammar School will become a 'living museum' where children can experience what school was like in the past. As the requirements for the restoration of the Old Grammar School are relatively straightforward it is hoped that work will begin in 2005. The Saracen's Head is already well used by local groups but this is to be increased by modifying the facilities and providing access for all. It is a very complex building and will require much consultation, designing, and planning before the work is put out to tender.

CATALOGUE OF SALE OF

Household Furniture & Effects

AT THE

Saracen's Head Inn

THE GREEN, KINGS NORTON

(Close to Tram and 'Bus route and within a few minutes' walk from
Railway Station).

MESSRS.

FOSTER & REDFERN, F.A.I.

(RODERICK & SON.   Established 1821.

Will Sell by Auction, by direction of the Executors of the late
Mr. GEORGE FREDERICK COOMBES, on the Premises as above,

On MONDAY, OCTOBER 19th, 1925

Commencing at **ELEVEN** o'clock prompt, the Useful **HOUSEHOLD**

FURNITURE

AND EFFECTS, including

Sheraton Mahogany Bedroom Suite

And Bedsteads, Bedding, Oak Wardrobe, Toilet Tables, Chests of Drawers,

OLD TALLBOY CHEST OF EIGHT DRAWERS

SPANISH MAHOGANY SIDEBOARD,   MAHOGANY EXTENDING
DINING TABLES, Marble & other Clocks, Overmantels, Easy & other Chairs

EXCELLENT PIANOFORTE

In Burr Walnut Case, by SAMES; Hall Stands, Oil Paintings, Prints, Contents
of Kitchen and Scullery, Large COPPER STOCK POT, Mahogany-framed
Seating, Two Lawn Mowers, Garden Tools and Miscellaneous Effects.

CATALOGUES may be obtained from Messrs. REYNOLDS & CO.,
Solicitors, 17, Waterloo Street ; or from the AUCTIONEERS, 50, Newhall
Street, Birmingham.

MOODY BROS., PRINTERS, BIRMINGHAM.

Furniture sale at the Saracen's Head, 19 October 1925. The local community has been
very keen both to use the building for meetings of the many social groups, and also to
raise funds to contribute to its upkeep.

A touring group of Morris dancers performed at the Saracen's Head in 1988. The scene reinforces the unique 'Englishness' of the village.

The dairy window at the Saracen's Head, 2002. The tithe map shows a 'dairy piece'. A window without glass would also have been exempt from tax.

The Saracen's Head's new sign, 2002. The History Society raised funds and obtained a grant for a new sign, which was designed and painted by Roger Simmons and features a Saracen's head on one side and the royal coat of arms on the other. It was unveiled in 1986 by Lord King's Norton, former local industrialist Harold Roxbee-Cox, who was educated at King's Norton Grammar School.

The Saracen's Head, 2002. Behind the Saracen's Head is a pathway known as Birdcage Walk. The brick wall was the boundary of the former Birdcage Farm.

The village pump and cottages in the churchyard, 1920s. The cottages and the pump were demolished and the lych gate now occupies the site. The notice on the pump states that the water is unfit for drinking. The cottages were at one time used as lodgings for curates.

The shop on the east side of the Green was built in the 1880s, and is seen here *c.* 1965. It was a sweet shop until the Second World War. Later it became the post office and then a photographer's premises. It is now a health products shop. The road running up to the church was previously known as 'Twatlin', a derivative of Watling Street, but there is no evidence of a connection with the Roman road.

The building on the east side at the top of Back Lane is now waiting for a further change of business. It is seen here in 2002.

Cottages on the north side of the Green, *c.* 1912. These had been malthouses. In the fifteenth century, when the village was developing, ale and small beer were safer to drink than the water. Tea and coffee were unknown beverages at that time.

This is one of the first shops of the Ten Acres & Stirchley Co-operative Society (TASCOS) on the Pershore Road. The first Co-operative shop for King's Norton was in Wharf Road. It became a Christian Science Reading Room when the new shop was opened in 1935. An extension that faces the Green and was used as a hairdressers was built in 1950. Above the shop is a hall that was used for parties and wedding receptions.

The shop on the corner of Pershore Road and Back Lane, 1960s. It has been a butcher's shop and a hairdressers, and is now Gascoigne's Funeral Services.

The TASCOS shop had an entrance on the east side of the Green, 1960s.

Lloyds Bank has been on this site since 1890, but the deeds held by the bank show that the building dates back to 1845 when it was in the name of Josiah Hands cordwainer, who was registrar and possibly also postmaster. There have been several alterations to the building, in particular moving the entrance from the Green to the Pershore Road. A flat above the bank was the home of the bank manager.

Lloyds Bank following alterations in 1947. Further changes have since taken place and the front entrance is now on the Pershore Road.

On the corner of the Redditch Road and the Green was Mortiboys sweet shop, built in 1896 and seen here in the 1940s. The shop and the house next to it were built on land that had been used as a coal-yard. Richard Foster built the shop for his daughter and her husband Alborn Mortiboys.

Agnes Regina Jenkins (left), mother of Janette Hourigan, with her sister Alice Maud Mortiboys, in the shop, 1940s. The Mortiboys are an old established family with connections to the Old Bell Inn and the cinema.

Ye Olde Bell Inn on the Green, 1907. The buildings at the side of the public house show further evidence of medieval construction. The record of a court case in 1820 states that 'The jury do present: the skittle alley lately made on the Green in the Village of King's Norton within the Manor aforesaid is a public nuisance.' In 1840 the Green was common land for free grazing, although it is suggested that bear-baiting and cock-fighting also took place during the nineteenth century. During the Second World War a large area of the Green was excavated to build two communal air raid shelters. It is believed that they are still there.

The Old Bell, *c*. 1900. In 1840 Richard Foster, who brewed his own beer, owned the Old Bell. There was extensive stabling behind the inn, suggesting that it was an old coaching inn. The Old Bell was sold to Southans Brewery in 1896 and closed in 1931, at which time Mitchells & Butlers owned it. It was divided into a shoe repairers and a private house. It has since been demolished.

Shops on the site of The Old Bell inn, 1982.

Motor cycle group outside Ye Olde Bell Inn, 1920s. For a long time King's Norton has had a motor cycle club. It was formed in August 1934, disbanded in late 1938 and restarted in December 1944. It is one of the longest established motor cycle clubs in the UK. The club head quarters was the Bull's Head for a short period in 1938, and later the Navigation Inn. From April 1945 to April

1969 the club met in the Hazelwell Hotel in King's Heath. It has a membership of 200 both active and non-active members, with an extensive age range. Interests include road racing, classic bikes, trials and moto-X, camping and moped racing. The club produces a monthly magazine, *The King's Norton Review*, and provides overseas members with a personal club link.

The rear of Hirons Bakery, showing Mrs Edkins, the owner, as a young girl riding a pony, *c.* 1930. The property is still owned by the young girl on the pony who now lives in a flat near her daughter in Herefordshire.

Hirons Bakery, 1960s. The 1840 tithe map shows that a shop was already established on this site. The deeds of the building go back to the beginning of the nineteenth century and refer to earlier deeds. It is believed to have been built in the seventeenth century but more recent investigation suggests it is earlier and may have been St Mary's Hall, the home of Chantry Priests. In the eighteenth century it was a smallholding. It has been extensively altered in the last decade but is considered to be the oldest building still standing in the village after the Saracen's Head. Windows in the flat that had been changed have now been restored. The end of the building, including the stairs, was demolished. There was a compulsory purchase order on land behind the bakery on which was built King's Norton's first police station.

Hirons Bakery was leased to Spar for a supermarket and is seen in 1993. Mrs Edkins' son-in-law, Keith Lealan, gave the History Society access to the flat above the supermarket. He provided further references to the ghost, possibly of a Chantry Priest. One of the family was having a bath and looked up to see the figure of a man sitting on the edge of the bath. Through the wide crack in the bedroom door Keith saw someone looking in the bedside cupboard. A former employee described an occasion when she had been working in the new outside building and looked up to see a man walking towards her. He didn't get any closer. Someone else saw a man walk through the wall of the same building.

James Melling examining the beams in the attic of the supermarket, 2004.

Evidence of the medieval origins and later extension of the supermarket, 2004.

Original beams inside the flat above the supermarket, 2004.

Every-body's Doin' it

With the people of Bournville galore,
Its the fashion to come to our Store,
To join with this band,
You drink 5 Crown Brand,
The pass-word you'll find is encore.

**5 Crown Brand
BRITISH SHERRY**

Oval	Bott	Oval	Flask	Nip
2/9	2/-	1/6	1/-	6d.
quart		pint		

TONIC & APPETISER

Also Wines for Weddings

**EMPIRE WINE & SPIRIT
STORES**
(D. AIREY, PROP.)

STIRCHLEY, KINGS NORTON
SELLY OAK and NORTHFIELD

A newspaper advertisement for Empire Wine & Spirit Stores, 1938.

An outing by horse and cart, from the Plumbers Arms, *c.* 1890. The Plumbers Arms was built in the eighteenth century. It remained open as a public house until 1931 when it became a fish and chip shop. In 1968 it was partly destroyed by fire and the upper storeys were removed. It was later demolished.

Outside the Plumbers Arms, 1900s.

The Plumbers Arms, by now a single-storey building, ceased operating in 1931. This picture dates from 1969; perhaps it was a barber's at this time.

Following total demolition of the Plumbers Arms, excavations on 5 November 1992 revealed evidence of a settlement dating back to the medieval period.

A new off-licence was built after demolition of the two cottages near the Plumbers Arms, 1960s.

Old Square, King's Norton, 1935. This was demolished to accommodate the cinema.

King's Norton cinema was owned by the Clifton Group. The Old Square was demolished in 1936 and a year later the cinema was built. There was considerable opposition to this as it was felt it would spoil the aspect of the Green. The cinema was described as: 'An imposing red-brick building with wide marble steps leading to the entrance and built (oddly) at one end of an English village green. Unusually seating and carpeting in both the stalls and the small circle were of a light green colour. Along with wall lighting, the cinema was lit by a series of decorative grilles in the ceiling that stretched the width of the cinema. The cinema had a large orchestra pit at the base of a very imposing oblong proscenium arch, complemented by what seemed huge travellers.' To combat the decline in cinema-going in the 1960s bingo was offered on Friday and Sunday evenings. Despite local opposition it was demolished in 1987. Kwik-save wanted to build a supermarket on the site. At a meeting with residents and Birmingham City Council there were claims this would cause traffic hazards. Fortune favoured the locals: while they were discussing the issues a car travelling from Westhill Road turned into the Green and crashed into a parked vehicle.

Grosvenor Court, sheltered flats that were built on the site of the cinema, 1988.

Fox's store, 1900s. This was a draper's shop on the north-west side of the Green, run by the Fox family. Hilda Woolley was the granddaughter of Minnie Fox and daughter of Alice Kerrison Fox. The locals called the shop 'General Fox's'.

Minnie Fox.

Alice Kerrison Fox,
born in 1886.

Fox's store, 1970s. It is now the Luxor Indian Restaurant.

The Old Cottages next to the Bull's Head, 1982. They were owned by Mitchells & Butlers and used as homes for retired landlords.

The Bull's Head, *c.* 1900. Thomas Chaplin was licensee of the old Bull's Head between 1880 and 1902. He kept an excellent nursery garden and was well known to local people for his horticultural skills. He sold it to Mitchells & Butlers who had it demolished, and the new Bull's Head was built in 1902. Some old cottages were cleared to create a car park. It underwent further alterations that were completed in 1989.

The Bull's Head, 2002.

2

The Surrounding District

Malcolm Beech outside his home, 1950s. The prefabs were made of compressed cardboard. The urgent need for housing after the Second World War was filled by the erection of prefabricated buildings. It was supposed to be a temporary situation for about ten years, but the buildings lasted a lot longer than that because so many of the tenants loved their homes. Druids Heath Estate was built in the mid-1960s to house tenants from Balsall Heath in a slum clearance project. There was no reference to Druids Heath in the tithe map but a Mr Drew owned property in the area and it is likely that the estate was named after him. The green fields are now gone, having been replaced by houses and tower blocks. The nearby Maypole public house was built in 1936 but is now disused and boarded up. It is a listed building so its future will be monitored, but there are no plans to develop it at present.

Alison Beech in the rural Maypole area before the Druids Heath Estate was built, 1950s.

An Anderson shelter now used as a garden shed, Maypole, 2004. Anderson shelters could be built in a day although the brickwork took longer to complete. They were usually below ground level with soil on the roof for disguise and to absorb the blast. There are still a number of them existing as garden sheds. Some people remember having a Morrison shelter (described as a strongly reinforced table) in their homes.

Monyhull Cottage, home of film star Brian Aherne in the 1930s. The De Lacey Aherne family were the architects of the mail houses built near the junction of Camp Lane and Pershore Road. There were two sons who became film stars. Brian Aherne was born in 1902 and died in 1986. He had roles in many films from *The Eleventh Commandment* in 1924 to *Rosie!* in 1967. He also made guest appearances in *Rawhide*, *The Twilight Zone* and *Crossroads*.

Monyhull Hall, 1950s. It is first mentioned in historic documents in 1608, although there was an earlier estate dating back to 1237 and reference to a watermill being built on the Chinn Brook in 1286. It was built by John Pountney in about 1760 and additions were made in the nineteenth century. The Sparring family of Monyhull along with others lost their houses because of their involvement in the Gunpowder Plot. In 1908 Monyhull Hall was bought by Birmingham Board of Guardians for use as a 'home for Epileptics and the Feeble Minded'. It is now a hospital and training centre for patients with learning difficulties.

The Junction, West Heath. The 'Bath Tub', a large lido, was one of West Heath's best-remembered features. It was part of the Laughton Works and was drained during the Second World War. Air-raid shelters were built, power presses took the place of the dressing cubicles, the fun fair became a packing department and the ice-cream parlour a workshop. The most significant product at the time was the assembly of Eddystone Communications Receivers that were dropped to Resistance groups during the war. The former lipstick plant was used for drawing primers for shells, and during the 1940 blitz they provided 31.5 million primers for the Ministry of Supply.

West Heath Hospital, 2003. The hospital in West Heath was known as the Fever Hospital in the 1920s and was where children suffering from scarlet fever were taken. When passing the hospital people covered their faces and held their breath to ensure they didn't catch anything.

Maundesley Hall, home of the Lane family, *c.* 1895. Squire Charles Pelham Lane was a prominent local man, a landowner and a magistrate.

Maundesley Hall during demolition in 1936. Near the hall is a barn. The type of brickwork used suggests it was built in the eighteenth century. When the barn was being demolished it was found to have a timber frame dating back to the seventeenth century. Further investigation revealed that the roof timbers had been recycled from an earlier building dating back to 1466–1501 and was therefore of a similar age to the buildings around the Green.

The Breedon Bar, 2002. Despite being a listed building the Breedon Bar had been damaged by fire and neglect that had made the building unsafe, and it would have cost Birmingham City Council an estimated £70,000 to put right. It was sold for a reported £420,000. The £1.8 million redevelopment consisted of twenty-four two-bedroom apartments for shared ownership from Waterloo Housing Association.

The Breedon Bar ready for demolition, 2003.

New flats on the site of the Breedon Bar, 2004.

Haye House at Breedon Cross, built in 1860 and photographed in 2003. Lifford was an early industrial area of King's Norton. Down the hill was the site of Guest, Keen & Nettlefolds. During the war a bomb hit the nearby Capon Heaton Company. There have been three Lifford stations. Signs of the old wharves still remain.

Cartland Arms, later the Sporting Parson, now McDonalds, 2003. The public house was named after one of the major landowning families. Ronald Cartland was the first Member of Parliament to be killed in the Second World War. The writer Barbara Cartland was related to the family. Excavation in the 1940s identified it as a former Roman site. Archaeological digs revealed Roman occupation between Parsons Hill and Lazy Hill, with finds of pottery, tiles, bricks and coins. Nearby was the Roman road called the Saltway, which led from Droitwich to Metchley Fort.

Lifford Hall, *c.* 1980. The hall and the area surrounding it have been the subject of research by George Demidowicz. There are indications of a Saxon settlement at a ford over the River Rea. There was a 1317 medieval mill that was possibly built on the site of an earlier chapel or monastic establishment. In 1768 the owner James Hewitt became Baron Lifford. Thomas Dobbs acquired Lifford including the house, mill and the surrounding land in 1807 but in 1810 he sold 7 acres of land for Lifford Reservoir. In 1860 a second mill on the bend of Tunnel Lane was converted from a rolling mill to rubber manufacture. The firm occupying the premises was G.R. Wilson & Co. J. & E. Sturge purchased it in 1948. In the 1950s Lifford Mill was demolished. The hall suffered serious vandalism and a fire in 1985. It has since been restored.

Lifford Hall in 1993 after restoration by George Demidowicz.

Almshouses on West Hill Road, 1960s. Two almshouses were built along Birdcage Walk in 1856. The almshouses were built sideways on to Westhill Road, between the new King's Norton Parish Hall and St Nicolas Gardens. They were endowed by Avenant's Charity to house two elderly ladies of the parish. By 1969 the houses had become damp and draughty and were demolished.

West Hill Road from the park entrance, 1984. There are now allotments in Westhill Road behind St Nicolas Gardens. During the 1940s the Revd Wilbert Awdry of 'Thomas the Tank Engine' fame lived in Westhill Road. Wilbert Awdry was curate at St Nicholas Church, and Sheila Neish recounts how during the war years he took his son and groups of other children to the station to watch the trains pass through. The stories he told Christopher during an illness later went on to become the 'Thomas the Tank Engine' books. He lived in Westhill Road when he wrote the first books, but had moved to East Anglia by the time they were published.

Hawkesley Hall gutted by fire, 1960s. The name dates back to when the king bred and trained hunting birds in the area. There was also a Hawkesley Farm and a Hawkesley House. One of the properties was the scene of the Battle of King's Norton during the Civil War.

View of the three estates, 2003.

An aerial view of the land for the proposed Hawkesley Estate, 1960s. An extract from Bournville Works magazine shows the reluctance of Cadburys to sell the land that was to provide essential homes for the overcrowded city dwellers: 'In 1936 the Firm bought the Moundesley Hall Estate and later offered it to the Corporation at the price paid for it, together with a gift of £20,000 if the Council would undertake to keep it, together with Primrose Hill and Hawkesley Hall Estates, as part of a permanent Green Belt for agricultural purposes or playing fields.' After very careful consideration we have decided to agree to the City Council's request to release from the covenant the 66 acres. We do so, however, with great reluctance and only upon the assurance that the remainder of the covenanted areas will be included in the official Green Belt Scheme'.

The density of the tower blocks led to problems of dampness, vandalism and social isolation: 'Despite their appealing names Primrose Hill, Pool Farm and Hawkesley represent the ward's most deprived estates. Cadbury's are giving their support to King's Norton and are devising an action plan to reduce anti-social behaviour, crime and drug use among local 10–16 year olds by a work placement programme, and apprenticeship opportunities.' The need to redesign parts of the estates is being addressed by the rehousing of tenants and the demolition of some of the tower blocks. The changes are being financed under a New Deal in the Community project with Lottery funding.

The Tunnel Cottages, above the entrance to the Wast Hill Canal Tunnel, 2002. The following year estate agents Dixons advertised one of the Tunnel Cottages for sale for £89,950. It was described as 'A cottage comprising lounge, dining room, utility, kitchen, upstairs bathroom, two bedrooms, storage heating (where specified), front and rear gardens.' These cottages stand above the mouth of the tunnel, and were built for canal workers. In 1849 they stood in lonely isolation with fields all around. They were recently renovated. The banks of the canal are now so overgrown that the mouth of the tunnel can only be seen from a boat.

Demolition of one of the tower blocks built in the 1970s. In the early 1960s the site now occupied by Primrose Hill Estate was meadow and pasture land. In 1930 Masshouse Farm had been demolished and the land used to build the Victoria estate. The designer of Primrose Hill council estate won an award from the Ministry of Housing and Local Government. The tower blocks that dominated the older buildings were not a success and after only thirty years are to be replaced with more appropriate housing.

Demolition of a tower block, 2004.

Prefabs in Rednal Road, 1960s. All the prefabricated buildings in King's Norton have since been demolished.

Wychall Farm and Overbury estates development, 1950s. In 1871 King's Norton had a nursery garden owned by Mr Henry Pope that supplied the Botanical Gardens. The Pope family named Overbury Road after the place they retired to. The roads on the estate were given the names of poets, hence the name of 'Poets' Corner'.

Opposite, left: A medieval boundary wall between King's Norton and Northfield, 1960s. Medieval hedges are being destroyed with considerable speed of removal, with claims of it having been done by accident or to improve the view. Wychall Road was a greenfield site developed in the 1930s. The golf course land was owned by the club members who sold it to Birmingham Corporation for £850,000 for housing development. The club moved to a new course at Weatheroak. This was the start of a vast council housing scheme that swept over the whole area. A big motor bridge replaced the little footbridge over the Rea, and all around tower blocks and other housing sprang up.

Kipling Road, 1950s. The estate was built across the boundary with neighbouring Northfield and is linked to the southern part of Wychall estate by Pope's Lane.

Kipling Road, 2003.

Longfellow Road flats, built in the 1950s. The author remembers her arrival at the flats that were home for seventeen years. The family had lived with grandparents in Hall Green. The road had not been metalled so it was a trudge through thick mud and clay. The flats inside were spacious and each had its own piece of garden. Coppers were earned for collecting leaves from the top of the lane to put on the garden as mulch. Train spotting was a favourite pastime, as well as cricket against the lamppost, marbles and skipping with a long rope. A bus took the children to Tiverton Road School until one was built at Wychall Farm.

Longfellow Road flats demolished, 2003.

Roadworks in Camp Lane, 1984. The Revd J.M.L. Aston, vicar of King's Norton, suggested that Camp Lane was the site of one of the outdoor settlements of the Danes and stated that traces of an encampment had been made out. It has also been said that this was the area where the Royalist troops camped on their way to join Prince Rupert, while Queen Henrietta Maria stayed at the Saracen's Head.

Nineteenth-century melting pots line the banks of the River Rea, 1984.

Allotments on the site of the mill pool in Camp Lane, 1996. Some fortunate city-dwellers had guinea gardens. These were large allotments of about ¼ acre on the Calthorpe Estate, for which workers paid rent of a guinea a year. Hurst Mill allotments are on the site of the Mill Pool in Camp Lane.

Alfred and Annie Astley selling their produce, grown in Camp Lane, in the Bull Ring, Birmingham, early 1900s. Annie Astley came from Badminton and married Alfred Astley. They had a stall in Birmingham's Bull Ring in front of the Home and Colonial Stores, where they sold flowers grown in a nursery in Camp Lane.

Last Chance Post leased to Mr Hickenbottom, formerly Maggie Riley's sweetshop, 2004.

An Edward VII letter-box in Station Road, 2004.

Pressall and Co. press toolmakers in a row of cottages in Camp Lane, shortly before demolition in the 1970s. Press toolmakers occupy all that remains of the row. There was also a general shop, the only one outside the village. The occupants of the cottages worked mainly at Wychall Rolling Mill, or on the Birmingham to Gloucester Railway which opened in 1840.

The original Camp Lane shop.

Hurst Mill and Mill House, 1986. According to the *Victoria County History* Henry Field left a mill called Hurste Mill to his niece Anne and her husband William Whorwood in 1584, and it was still in their family in 1625. The mill stands at a point on the River Rea where grist mills have stood for hundreds of years, probably from the sixteenth century or earlier. The present Hurst Mill probably dates from the eighteenth century and was the last working water mill in Birmingham. In 1940, after ten years of negotiations, the Public Works Department of the Corporation was recommending acceptance of an agreement with the mill owner to purchase the land. They wanted to carry out improvements to both the river and Camp Lane, and to make an open space.

The Mill House belonging to George Attwood, *c.* 1965.

Entrance to the King's Norton Business Centre, 2003. Slough Estates now own what was formerly the King's Norton Factory Centre. It was once notable as a safe place to teach learner drivers. Birmingham Mint had a factory here where they minted commemorative coins. In 1901 a Century Commemorative medal was minted for its employees, as was the King's Norton penny in 1918–9 which is distinguished by the initials KN beside the date. It became part of Nobel Industries Ltd in 1918 and helped to found Imperial Chemical Industries Ltd in 1926. Coins were last made with a King's Norton mintmark in the early 1970s. Another significant company was BKL Alloys, founded by three German Jews who were escaping persecution. The company created materials for planes during the war and afterwards theirs was one of the few foundries that could recycle the metal that contained magnesium. The Germans were interred on the Isle of Man for the duration of the war. The company had a connection with Kurt Hahn, who founded Gordonstoun School and whose son was a roommate of Prince Philip. Mary Rose, who worked there for twenty-three years, reported an occasion when Prince Philip arrived in a helicopter to see Oscar Hahn.

Pershore Road near Camp Lane, 1938. On the Pershore Road side of the junction are the Mail houses. The project was to give high-quality builders like Grants the opportunity to show that good homes could be built in very short periods of time. Building began in November 1919 and the first of the six houses was occupied in December, with the remainder being completed in January 1920.

Pershore Road under its former name of Church Hill, 1900s.

The meeting of the roads from the church tower, 1900s.

The Provident Chapel at the five ways junction, 1960s. This was the building on the junction of Redditch Road and Masshouse Lane. It ceased to be used as a chapel before the First World War but its shape and windows make its origins obvious. It was not actually shown on the 1840 map but it bore a plaque to the effect that it was built in 1838 and was the first Methodist chapel in the area. It later became a newsagent's shop. Beyond the chapel was the Old Mews livery stable and on the opposite side of Masshouse Lane were two shops and a row of cottages. Masshouse Farm is said to be one of the houses where secret masses were held during the Reformation. After the destruction of their property the Franciscan fathers had to seek shelter in places where they might hope to escape the fury of the times (1688–9).

Five Ways junction, 1920s. Just beyond the Provident Chapel was the Old Mews livery stable. It was a stables and later a garage owned by the Webb family. Horses and horse-drawn carriages could be hired from here. The presence of such an enterprise indicates that King's Norton was an affluent area at this period.

Wharf Road sale ground, *c.* 1890. This was an enclosure on the corner of Wharf Road and Pershore Road South where stray cows and horses were gathered. A cattle market was held there on alternate Wednesdays. It was discontinued in 1927, but is well remembered by the older people of King's Norton. The village was granted its first market in 1616 by James I. In 1840 the buildings behind the pound were coal and lime wharves and stabling belonging to the Birmingham & Worcester Canal Company.

Navigation Inn, 1960s. This was next to the Sale Ground and presumably dated and took its name from the nearby canal. The new Navigation Inn replaced it in 1906. Behind the public house was an area called the Lakin. The Mop had been held there and the gypsy in her caravan was also remembered.

The first Co-operative store was built at the same time as the new Navigation Inn. It became the Christian Science Reading Room until their chapel was built.

The Christian Science Chapel, 1960s. This has since been replaced by Rowan Court sheltered bungalows.

Shephard's Yard in Wharf Road, 1920s and '30s. The Shephard family ran a wheelwrighting and blacksmithery business in King's Norton from 1877 until 1960, first next to the Bull's Head on the Green and later at the Alpha Farm in Wharf Road. The full report of Stephen Price's research into the business is reported in the *Birmingham Historian*, no. 6.

The Alpha Farmhouse, dating from 1800. The construction of the house was interesting as, although filled in with brickwork, it rested on oak beams from the ground level, cross-section oak beams at first floor level, and roof beams from bent oaks. In the kitchen was a deep well with a wooden pump, and a flash oven with brewing coppers. The buildings were demolished following a compulsory purchase order.

Buildings belonging to the canal company included coal and lime wharves, and stabling, 1960s. The buildings were made into living accommodation. Nearby is the Baptist chapel. It was built in 1847 to replace two end cottages, one of which was formerly used as the chapel. A third cottage, purchased at the same time, became the vestry and classroom. A front wall was added to match the rest of the buildings. On 15 October 1922 King's Norton was formed into a separate church (from Canon Street Church). The canal has been used as a baptistery. At one ceremony several of the congregation slipped and fell into the water.

Former canal buildings for the coal and lime wharves, 2003.

Wharf Road looking towards the Green, 1910.

Harry and Charlotte Sharp's 'pop' shop on the canal, 1936. The actual site of this shop is uncertain.

Cottage by the canal, 2004. Until 1915 the white building next to it was a beerhouse. It has been converted into cottages.

Outside the beerhouse on the canal towpath by Wharf Road Bridge.

3

Farms & Industry

Wychall Farm, probably dating from the fourteenth century, 1950s. The southern farms of King's Norton did not disappear until after the Second World War when they became municipal housing estates. Free trade and cheaper imported grain meant more unemployment for farmers, millers and various other traders. The building of the railway, other industrial development and the need to provide houses for the workforce had reduced the area of farmland. In 1925 the Pardoes, who owned the farm, took in lodgers – which suggests that the economic viability of arable farming was ending. Birmingham City Council bought the land in the 1950s to build a new housing estate.

Wychall Farm with extensions dated 1770–80, seen in the 1950s.

Tenants of Wychall Farm, *c.* 1925.

Tenants of Wychall Farm, 1900s.

An aerial view of Bell's Farm, 1901. Steve Bond, curator, has written a brief and very interesting history of Bell's Farm. A moated farmhouse is described in Domesday Book but there is evidence of much earlier occupation in the area. The site enjoyed good views of the surrounding countryside and the hunting of deer and wild boar would have been good. In the seventeenth century the estate passed from the Middlemore family to the Field family. During the Civil War it passed from the Royalist William Field to his son Edward who supported Cromwell. Improvements to the building included the addition of the ornate fluted chimneystacks, one of which bears the date 1661. The 1848 Tithe Schedule shows new hedges being planted, suggesting that the existing hedges could have been medieval.

At the beginning of the twentieth century the building was used as the farm manager's house for the farming operation to support the Monyhull Colony. In the 1930s there was a considerable expansion of local housing as the slum clearances of the city swallowed up the countryside. Arable farming was intensified during the Second World War. The last tenants moved out in 1976 and vandalism and the threat of demolition led to the forming of the Bell's Farm Community Association. In 1980 the building was badly damaged in a fire. Reconstruction began with funding from the Manpower Services Commission's Community Programme. The pebbledash cladding to the front of the building was not included in the restoration. Today, Bell's Farm is run jointly as a community and educational resource centre and is host to a diverse range of users, from uniformed youth activities through schools use to a Dark Age Historical Re-enactment group and as a venue for live role-play game events.

Bell's Farm, 1901.

Bell's Farm, 2004.

The living quarters of the tenant farmer, 1970s.

Bell's Farm roof space before restoration.

The sixteenth-century Primrose Hill Farm, working until the 1970s, is seen *c. 1973*. Primrose Hill Farm is Grade II listed and was formerly known as Hole Farm. It was mentioned in the late fifteenth century Court Rolls of the Manor of Bromsgrove and King's Norton as the home of a branch of the Field family. In 1864 the farmstead owned just over 82 acres of land enclosed before 1772–4. From the eighteenth century the farm was defined on at least three sides by sunken lanes bordering medieval estates. A survey by the Birmingham University Field Archaeology Unit confirmed that the buildings include a fifteenth-century timber-framed farmhouse that was constructed on an artificial platform. The site also has a well-preserved seventeenth-century barn that is a four-bay timber-framed structure of post and truss construction.

The farm's more recent history and its future are unclear. It was reported that Birmingham City Council sold it for £9,000 to a councillor who went bankrupt and absconded. For a period it functioned as a garden centre. In the mid-1970s the *Evening Mail* investigated a report that devil worshipping was being carried out. An advertisement on 24 October 1980 asked for freehold offers for 'A valuable and historic timber framed Farmhouse and Barn dating back to the fifteenth century set in approximately 1.7 acres'. The farm is now hemmed in by council and private housing. A local group is active in securing its future.

Pool Farm, 1951. Little has been recorded about the farms and the families who once worked the land in the area. There is evidence of a significant agricultural heritage with sites indicating strip farming, and ridge and furrow. The spoil from cutting the canal changed the landscape by creating the mounds on the Hawkesley estate. The growth of the city and slum clearance projects created the need for land on which to build homes. Rural King's Norton was an inevitable target for development. Three estates were built and given the names of the farms they replaced. They were not a total success. There is now a community development trust, funded through the government's New Deal for Communities project with a budget of £50 million over ten years, that has the aim of making the three estates an area in which people want to live and work.

Brandwood Farm, 1929. In 1900 the estate of Brandwood was in the ownership of George Frederick Lyndon JP.

Dawberry Fields Farm, King's Heath, *c.* 1930.

Blackgreve Farm was recorded on the 1840 tithe map and its moat suggests it has medieval origins.

There were several Malt House Farms and one remains in the area now occupied by the Cocks Moors Woods Sports Centre and golf course.

Rowheath Farm, c. 1910. It was previously called Griggs' Farm. Although it is now a housing estate the barn can still be seen. There are many happy memories of the lido that once occupied the site.

Newhouse Farm was located to the west of the village of King's Norton. In 1840 its owner was Robert Edward Eden Mynors, and the tenant was John Phillips. The farm consisted of buildings, yards, garden and foredrove. A foredrove is a farm track.

Traditional methods of farming and ploughing the fields were being used in the early twentieth century.

Ploughing the fields was a family event. School records show that children were involved in harvesting and therefore went absent from school.

Basic foodstuffs like this potato crop were farmed for local use.

This may well be a 'nightsoil man' who collected waste from earth closets and 'miskins', and used it as fertiliser on farmland, early 1900s.

River Rea flood control in Popes Lane, 2002. The Rea rises from the Lickey Ridge watershed. Floods have been a characteristic of the Rea Valley, influencing the road pattern but also supporting a significant number of mills.

Wychall Mill. Mills had been sited along the River Rea from Saxon times. The first known and surviving reference to a mill at Wychall is contained in a deed of 1638. The mills would originally have been for grinding corn. A leat was constructed from the stream along the valley side to give the necessary fall of water, and by the use of sluices the mill could be safeguarded against flooding. With the growth of industrialisation came a change in the use of mills. The rolling mill became the machine on which the Birmingham trades depended. The tithe map of 1840 identifies Wychall Mill as a rolling mill that was owned by Charles Emery. He sold it to Charles Ellis & Sons in the 1840s. A steam engine was introduced of the type invented by James Watt. By the end of the nineteenth century they had become large-scale manufacturers. In 1927, between the mill and the railway, Triplex built their precision works making glass for car windows, windscreens and aeroplanes. This company is now Pilkingtons Aerospace, accessed by the Catesby Business Park. In 1938 Burman's built a factory that produced copper-plated machine components for the motor industry. The mill complex became derelict in the 1950s and it was demolished in the 1970s.

Wychall Reservoir, 2002. Concern of the River Rea mill-owners over water supply resulted in conflict over water rights. To overcome this the construction of reservoirs was authorised in 1808. The reservoir was constructed on Wychall farmland that had a history of flooding. Walkway and cycle routes have been established and the area is now a nature reserve.

Wychall Reservoir with Pilkingtons Aerospace in the background, 2003.

King's Norton Brick Company. Keith Ackrill has done some research into the brick company. The site for the brick and tile works is recorded on a 1903 map of King's Norton. The Hough family who called in Alan Rollason to improve performance, owned it. During the Second World War the Luftwaffe used the twin chimneys as navigation points en route to the Austin Motor Works at Longbridge. In the 1950s the company, owned by the Atkins brothers, again called on Alan Rollason to improve business performance. The weekly target was for the production of 200,000 bricks and 20,000 on Saturdays. If the targets were not met the men had to work overtime. The company closed in 1958. The company used clay from local pits and Bryants, the housing giants, bought products from the KN brickworks. Cyril Hoff was a manager of the company and lived in Beak's Hill Road where he had stables for his horses.

King's Norton Brick Company's twin chimneys.

King's Norton Brick Company, derelict ground, 2004.

The former Baldwins Paper Mill, 2003. Baldwins Paper Mill began as Sherborne Mill. It was started by James Baldwin in 1836 and finally closed in 1965. It produced paper bags and gun wadding. Fortunately the buildings were not demolished but converted for other use. Initially it was the home of the Patrick Collection of vintage cars. While this venture achieved a lot of interest it was not economically viable. The site is now home to the Lakeside Centre and Lombard Rooms.

The former Baldwins Paper Mill, 2003.

Patrick Motors Collection, displayed in the former Baldwins Paper Mill.

Lifford Reservoir, 1932. In 1810 Thomas Dobbs, owner of the house and mill, sold 7 acres of land for the construction of Lifford Reservoir. The water was used to sustain the level of the canal. It became a tranquil place in an industrial area with its boathouse and tea-room, and was also a place for fishing. It remains a very peaceful area but the facilities have gone.

Speciality Minerals kiln tower, 2003. After the church spire the other landmark on the skyline is the 150-foot tall tower belonging to Speciality Minerals Ltd. The tower is actually a kiln where high-quality limestone, from Derbyshire, is reduced into the compounds used in pills and paper. Joseph Sturge founded the chemical works that has continued on the site despite changes of ownership.

4

Canals & Railways

Junction House, 1960s. According to Frank T. Lockwood the Junction House at
Lifford was the original headquarters of the Worcester & Birmingham Canal
Company. Built in 1796 it is where the Birmingham & Stratford Canal forms a
junction with the Birmingham & Worcester Canal. Various uses have been suggested
for the house from canal keeper's cottage, toll cottage, and even an inn. However,
local people identify the Junction Inn with a house that formerly stood near the
Guillotine Stop Lock. The first section of the canal from King's Norton to Hockley
Heath was opened in 1796. Only when the Dudley No. 2 Canal (Lapal Canal) was
completed and coal became readily available from the Black Country did work
restart. There was a lot of argument about tolls for traffic leaving one canal and
joining the other. It reached Wootton Wawen in 1813.

Junction House, 2003.

Junction House showing charges, 2003. Canals were able to transport heavy loads more quickly and cheaply than horses and carts. More ready access to coal and the use of steam power enabled pockets of industry to expand very rapidly. The number of people involved in the nail-making industry suggests that their products were not just for the local community and the canals were used for supplying the iron and then distributing the finished products. The rolling mill and chemical works that were within walking distance of the village acquired their materials by canal. Cadburys used canals to transport milk from the farms for chocolate. Produce and manufactured goods could be transported at more competitive prices. The canal boats were also an early form of transport for people from the city to come on outings to the countryside. In the late eighteenth and early nineteenth centuries Birmingham people would travel by barge along the Birmingham & Worcester Canal to attend the King's Norton 'Mop'. The return fare from Chapell's Wharf in Birmingham to King's Norton was 1 shilling.

Entrance to Wast Hill tunnel, 2003. Tunnels were usually built by laying out the straight route across the hilltop and then sinking a number of shafts. These were aligned on the surface using a telescope. Digging began in both directions from the bottom of all shafts, and from the tunnel entrances. Surveying techniques were basic at first, using plumblines. The early tunnellers were miners, who were not used to taking accurate headings, so the horizontal shafts sometimes didn't meet up correctly. Few early tunnels had towpaths, so the horse or donkey would walk over the top and the crew, possibly with some local helpers, would 'leg' the boat through, pushing with their feet against the tunnel sides or roof. Some tunnels had ropes or chains connected to the walls to pull the boats through. The Wast Hill tunnel runs from King's Norton to Hopwood and is a legging tunnel 2,726 yards long. Building started in 1794 and it was completed in 1797. There were difficulties in its construction. The navvies were in and around King's Norton for some time; they were not popular in spite of the trade they brought to the public houses. The Hawkesley mounds were created from spoil from the canal. Because of its length airshafts had to be constructed for ventilation. A track was made for the canal horses to be walked to the other end of the tunnel.

Although the banks of the canal are very overgrown the canal is still in use, but for pleasure rather than commerce. During the summer it was possible to take a trip from King's Norton to Tardibigge, with its many locks, going through the long Wasthill Tunnel. Motor-driven barges were licensed to supply food and drink, making it a very pleasant outing.

Guillotine lock, Lifford, *c.* 1960.

Guillotine lock, 2003.

Opposite, bottom: Guillotine lock, showing the tollhouse and the old road bridge, *c.* 1965. Officially the Guillotine lock was built to prevent the loss of water from one canal to the other. Locally its main purpose was considered to be to prevent barges from passing until the toll had been paid. Before 1814 there were double gates across the width of the canal, but it was narrowed to collect tolls.

Drawbridge Tunnel Lane, 1918. The crossing at Tunnel Lane is significant as a battleground for rights of passage to both the canal and the track. The early drawbridge was destroyed by fire and replaced with a fixed bridge, as the canal was no longer in use. The growth of the leisure industry and the pressure to restore canals resulted in conflict between the owners of the canal, those who wished to navigate the canal and those who wanted access from Tunnel Lane to Brandwood. The saga ran in the 1940s as intrepid boaters challenged the Great Western Railway's right to extinguish navigation on the canal at Lifford. The first of these was L.T.C. Rolt, famous for writing about canals and railways, whose exploits in navigating his boat *Cressey* is documented in his book *Landscape with Canals*. A swing bridge brought across from the Kennet & Avon Canal replaced the former fixed bridge. Following vandalism the bridge was secured to the bank to allow traffic on the canal. Since new roads in the area took traffic away from Tunnel Lane the bridge has lain derelict. However, the Ramblers' Association now wants an ancient pathway to be reopened.

Swingbridge Tunnel Lane, 2003.

Brandwood Tunnel, 2003. Brandwood Tunnel is King's Norton's second canal tunnel. It is 352 yards long and there were ropes to pull the barges through. Above the entrance there is a circular plaque to William Shakespeare, reminding us that this is the Birmingham to Stratford Canal.

The Old Canal Bridge at Millpool Hill. There was an old wharf here similar to the one at Hockley Heath, except that this wharf existed to serve local limekilns. Near the bridge overnight mooring was possible. With the increasing amount of traffic and the need for road widening the old bridge had to be replaced.

The New Canal Bridge at Millpool Hill.

The Camp public house, seen in 2003, was formerly called the New Railway Inn. Its name was changed in the belief that it overlooked the site where the Royalist troops camped during the Civil War. A medieval fireplace and surrounds suggest that a much earlier structure had once been on the site. There were once stables that have been removed, indicating that it had been a coaching inn.

Station Road level crossing, 1923.

Station Road, 2003. The railway enabled the middle classes to move away from the industrialised city to the cleaner outskirts from where they could commute. An act authorising the building of the Birmingham to Gloucester line was passed in 1836. The incline at Lickey was initially a source of concern but this was overcome, and by 1840 the line to Camp Hill was open. An embankment was constructed to take the railway across a large section of the Rea Valley, which divided the land belonging to Wychall Farm. Pope's Lane Bridge was built to link both sides of the new estate that was built in the 1950s. Both this bridge and the others at Cotteridge and Lifford have been extended as more tracks were laid.

King's Norton station, 1900s. Research by John Bachelor into the buildings of the station suggests that parts of it could have been built in about 1850, making it one of the earliest stations in Birmingham. During the Second World War hospital trains parked in King's Norton station sidings ready for the trip to the coast to collect casualties.

The 1957-built 'Park Royal' pauses at King's Norton centre platform on its service to Redditch. No. 44775 waits to use the crossover. *(P. Shoesmith)*

Ex-LMS 8F no. 48393 in a very work-stained condition crosses to take the Camp Hill line with a train of timber, 16 June 1963. *(P. Shoesmith)*

Ex-GWR 2800 class takes the Camp Hill line with a mixed freight cargo. The third van has a tarpaulin over a leaky roof, 18 March 1963. (*P. Shoesmith*)

Ex-LMS 4F no. 44333 passes a fine array of notices at King's Norton, 8 April 1961. It is a train of loco coal bound for the Austin Works at Longbridge. *(P. Shoesmith)*

Ex-Southern Railway 'Battle of Britain' class 34079 141 Squadron passes King's Norton with a Birmingham-bound train, 15 June 1964. *(P. Shoesmith)*

Diesel train passing through King's Norton, 2003. Myra Dean, the yardmaster's daughter, tells childhood memories of racing up and down the goods yard on her three-wheeled bike. The slope from the cattle pen was good for tobogganing down in winter. Early September brought the pigeon train to the end siding: nine or ten carriages would be filled with baskets of pigeons and it was one man's job to stay on this train to feed, water and release them at prearranged times. The siding in the goods yard was a good viewing point for watching the Triplex play cricket and football. On one bitterly cold occasion Myra, with her father, got into a train to watch the match in comfort. During the second half the train started to move. She wonders how they managed to jump off without breaking a limb. During dry summers the Fire Brigade were frequent visitors as sparks from the trains would ignite the grassy bank on Platform 1 and the bank at the bottom of the gardens of houses in Redwood Road.

5

Community & Social Life

King's Norton fire station, Cotteridge, 1992. The first fire station for the King's Heath and King's Norton volunteer Fire Brigade had a substation at 1 Holly Road that used to be manned by Mr Cox. A new fire station was built on the site of allotments at Cotteridge. At the side of the station an avenue of trees is all that remains of High House.

King's Norton and King's Heath Fire Brigade.

King's Norton Guides at Birmingham fire station, 1927.

The first King's Norton Guide Company, 74th Birmingham, was formed in 1922–3. Back row, left to right: Phyllis Stallard, Muriel Dix, Ivy Burgin, Alice Longford, Jessie Rickett, Mollie Stanford, Marjorie Hirons, Marjory Hayward, Gwen Johnson, Winnie Wort. Third row: Freda Mickle, Ruby Smith, Florence Tilley, Phyllis Manson, Edith Prickett, Dorothy Hemms, Clara Wakeman. Second row: Hettie Butcher, Elsa Manson, Agnes Garratt (captain), Winnie Round, Millie Morgan. Front row: Kathleen Prickett, Katie Armstrong, Margery Hucknell, Gwen Tye, Queenie Smith, Louise Cutler.

The Lord Mayor, Alderman Frank Price, being introduced to the King's Norton Scouts and Cubs by the Revd E.G. Ashford in 1964.

King's Norton Prize Band, 1911–12.

King's Norton Bowls Clubhouse, 2003. It was built in 1862 and is now Triplex pensioners' club. Kenneth Horne, who became a director of Triplex Glass Company, demonstrated gramophones from his shop in Cotteridge at the church hall, where he attended dances with his wife.

Bowling green at the back of the Saracen's Head, *c.* 1925.

King's Norton Bowls Club, *c.* 1900.

The Saracen's Head Bowls Team, between the wars.

King's Norton Youth Fellowship, 1955.

Front cover of *The Spire*, the magazine of the King's Norton Youth Fellowship. After several unsuccessful attempts to form a Youth Fellowship, in 1949 the Revd E.G. Ashford challenged a group of boys and girls to set up and run a club under their own jurisdiction for a trial period of three months. Three main principles were determined at the beginning. These were: (a) The committee would be in complete control and no outside authority would be permitted to dictate policy. (b) The King's Norton Youth Fellowship, as it was then named, would not deprecate any religious or political beliefs. Its only *bias* was towards the St Nicolas Parish Church to which it was affiliated. It was contended that both the church and the youth club would benefit if young people came to church via the youth club rather than vice versa. (c) The King's Norton Youth Fellowship would cater not only for the entertainment of its members but also for their education and well-being. It would not be a dancing and table tennis club as are so many of the clubs which have failed.

   John Hill and Philip Haycock accepted the challenge and a committee was formed with Alan Sharp as chairman. The success of the project was evidenced by the Christmas party at which 117 members sat down to a three-course meal. Having created the club it was sustained with various social functions and its magazine.

King's Norton Youth Club, 1960–1.

Saturday morning entertainment for children was given at the Picturedrome in Hudson's Drive, seen in 1992. The cost to the children was one penny. If the projector broke down during the show, as happened frequently, they would be told to line up and would get their money back. Sometimes they would be given a metal token to gain free admission for another show. Mr Calvert was the manager and Mrs MacDonald assisted him on the piano, her place sometimes taken by Mr Taft, the blind harmonium player. Local tradesmen advertised their wares on the curtain that was wound up and down between shows. At adult performances Sergeant Dawns, a veteran of the Crimean War, would recite the 'Charge of the Light Brigade', much to the patrons' delight.

An advertisement for the Savoy from the *Birmingham Times*, 19 August 1938.

The former Savoy cinema, now an engineering works, seen in 2004. Mr Calvert took over as manager of the cinema. He died when he fell through the roof doing some building work.

King's Norton Youth Fellowship hockey team in King's Norton Park, March 1952. The park was laid out when King's Norton became part of Birmingham. It was bought by Birmingham Civic Society in 1920 to save it from development and subsequently presented to the city. It offered tennis courts, a bowling green, a putting green and pitches for football, hockey and cricket, as well as grass areas and flower beds: a barometer of happier times. It became a vandalised, litter-ridden eyesore with an illegal caravan camp. The vandalised tennis courts have now gone, as have the changing rooms. Tree planting has taken place and it is becoming attractive once more.

King's Norton Park, July 1950. The buildings in King's Norton Park were changing rooms and greenhouses. In 1946 prefabs were built in the park as a temporary measure to alleviate the shortage of housing. They were removed in 1968 and the area was restored to the park.

King's Norton Park tennis group, 1952.

King's Norton Park today. The tennis courts have gone to grass.

6

Schools & Entertainment

King's Norton Primary School, 1970s. A school board was set up following the Education Act of 1870. In 1876 a Boys School with a headmaster, one teacher and forty-four boys, along with a Girls and Infants School with a headmistress and three teachers, were opened. The Old Grammar School was closed. The new schools could not accommodate all the children so in 1882 the School Board Offices were reorganised into a Boys and Girls Mixed School, with a separate Infants' School. Entries for absence in the school logbooks for the 1870s show that while education could wait the harvest couldn't. For example: 'Difficulty in getting children to school this week, haymaking in the parish'; 'School closed for Harvest holidays'; 'Many absent gathering bilberries'; 'Guardians of the Poor refuse to pay the fees of a boy. They consider he is old enough to work although he is but eleven'; 'Could not carry little sister to school. They live more than three miles away'.

By 1900 there were 244 children in the Mixed School and 217 in the Infants School. The overcrowding was partially overcome by the opening of Cotteridge School. The new Junior School building was opened in 1901 and the old building was refurbished for the Infants.

King's Norton Primary School pupils.

King's Norton Primary School pupils, 1936.

King's Norton Primary School coronation re-enactment, 1937.

King's Norton Nursery School was built in response to the 1944 Education Act. The well-equipped and well-run school became a target for vandals. The photograph shows the school, which is in Westhill Road, in the 1960s.

King's Norton Secondary School was built in 1958 with extensive grounds and games facilities. In the evenings it was used as an Institute of Further Education. It is now Cadbury College and a Centre for New Deal Training. It is pictured here before 1970.

Wychall Farm Junior School Skittleball Team, *c.* 1959. The building of the estate on the former farmland created the need for a school. Wychall Farm Junior and Infant Schools were built in 1956–7. By 1961 it accommodated fourteen classrooms but the estimated need was inaccurate and an annexe had to be provided. St Thomas Aquinas Catholic School now occupies the site of the former annexe.

MORNING
Commencing 9.45

9.45. BEAUTY QUEEN COMPETITION
(age from 16 years)

10.15. PLANT TREE FOR COMMEMORATION
(oldest tradesman)

10.30. DECORATED DOLL'S PRAM PARADE (Girls)

11.0. DECORATED CYCLE PARADE (Boys)

11.30. COMICAL DOG SHOW. (Thoroughbreds barred)

★

EVENING
Commencing 6.0 p.m.

6.0. OX ROAST
Roasted by Mr. P. RANDLE, of Pavilion Garage, Stirchley.
First slice will be cut by the oldest inhabitant
OX WILL BE DISTRIBUTED FREE

6.30. ANKLE COMPETITION

7.0. KNOBBLY KNEES COMPETITION

7.30. TARZAN COMPETITION

FREE DONKEY RIDES ALL DAY
(Gift Coun. ROB PRYKE)

GREASY POLE COMPETITION (20/- prize)
(to be run all day)

SPOT THE MYSTERY MAN
(He will be a tradesman from around the Green)
Correct method—" YOU are the mystery man,
I claim the prize."

JUDGING THE BEST DECORATED STREET

JUDGING THE BEST DECORATED SHOP
(around the Green)

SPOT THE ODD OBJECT IN THE SHOP WINDOWS
(around the Green)
Competition to run from May 26th till June 2nd.

ALL BABIES BORN ON CORONATION DAY WILL
RECEIVE 20/-
(In the defined area only)

WILSON'S GIGANTIC FUN FAIR

𝕲𝖔𝖉 𝕾𝖆𝖛𝖊 𝕿𝖍𝖊 𝕼𝖚𝖊𝖊𝖓

Coronation Mop programme, 1953.

The Mop was traditionally held on the Green and inevitably a lot of damage was done to the grass. Some of the locals objected and insisted on the Green being surrounded with posts and chains. The Mop was moved to Town Field behind the Old Square, and later to the Sale Ground where the car park for the Navigation Inn is now. Two other venues, the Lakin and Paper Mill Fields, were also used. In 1953 local traders revived the Mop to celebrate the Coronation of Queen Elizabeth II. The Mop returned to its traditional home, roads were closed, and it was a great success. In 1969 members of King's Norton Round Table took over much of the running of the Mop. The Mop is now Birmingham's sole surviving street fair. (*This account of the Mop was taken from Janette Hourigan's dissertation.*)

The Mop was authorised to hold a Court of Pie Powder – derived from old French 'Pied Poudre' a term used of traders, meaning dusty feet. It was used to tame the behaviour of traders, stallholders and 'cutpurses' (pickpockets) and thieves. Anyone found guilty could be fined or put in the stocks or pillories. In James I's reign began a craze of witch-hunts, people's fear of the devil's disciples. Any type of mark on the body was evidence of this, and the women who were found guilty were burned or hanged. In a petition by John Field, Bailiff and Yeoman 'seized the goods of Anne Wathan and Jane Smith as they were accused of witchery. They were tried, found guilty and put to death' – possibly on the village green.

Five Ways island decorated for the coronation celebrations, 1937.

Celebrating the coronation of Edward VII, 1902. Mitchells & Butlers provided window-boxes for all the cottages in order to beautify the village for the coronation of George V in 1910.

ACKNOWLEDGEMENTS

King's Norton History Society's committee and members have been magnificent in contributing photographs, documents and the information necessary to compile this book. The collections of Helen Goodger, C.A.P. Rogers and others are held by the Society. The staff at local libraries and the Local Studies Department of the Central Library have been very supportive. Chris Bowen in the Parish Office has been a source of much information. Local people and those with roots in King's Norton have all contributed. Special thanks are due to Frances Hopkins for her support, Kath Watts for allowing the use of her vast collection of photographs, and the three unpublished studies of King's Norton by Jan Hourigan, Val Fletcher and Maurice Robinson. Steve Bond, Philip Haycock, Keith Ackrill, Greta Lacey, Mary Rose, Hilda Woolley, James Melling, Claire Simpson, Jim Hyland, John and Jean Smith, Les Orton, and many others have made other contributions. Myra Dean provided personal information about the station. Geoff Dowling printed photographs taken by Peter Shoesmith and gave his permission as trustee of the collection for them to be included. Ray Aldington, the Ringing Master, had several additional climbs up the church tower to provide information about the bell ringing. Keith Lealan provided access to the medieval flat and attic of what was once Hirons Bakery.